Fabulous Fishing Funnies

Fabulous Fishing Funnies

JONNY HAWKINS

Skyhorse Publishing

Skyhorse Publishing books may be purchased in bulk at special discounts for sales promotion, corporate gifts, fund-raising, or educational purposes. Special editions can also be created to specifications. For details, contact the Special Sales Department, Skyhorse Publishing, 307 West 36th Street, 11th Floor, New York, NY 10018 or info@skyhorsepublishing.com.

Skyhorse® and Skyhorse Publishing® are registered trademarks of Skyhorse Publishing, Inc.®, a Delaware corporation.

Visit our website at www.skyhorsepublishing.com.

10 9 8 7 6 5 4 3 2

Library of Congress Cataloging-in-Publication Data is available on file.

Cover design by Owen Corrigan
Cover image by Jonny Hawkins

Print ISBN: 978-1-62914-750-5
Ebook ISBN: 978-1-62914-943-1

Printed in the United States of America

"Fishing without a license, Sarge."

"They've got Uncle Harry. . . . Quick, get the boat license number!"

"I caught it with an inchworm."

"The fish is fine to keep, Todd. What needs to be thrown back is the Snoopy pole."

"Be honest, Frank, you've never gone fishing for crappies before, have you?"

Jed's method of letting everyone know when he'd caught another keeper was beginning to get annoying.

When weakfish work out

Carps and robbers

**When commercial fishermen have had too
many viewings of the movie, *Titanic***

"Oar d'oeuvre?"

"Well, I guess I better throw *this* one back."

Bill logged on, working the net. After several hours online, he worried that he may have obtained a suspicious worm.

Albert is a basket case.

A balanced diet

"Forget it. I don't take plastic."

"I either go for low-life worms or I'm a sucker for jerkbait."

Speed bump

"Bucket o' crank bait, please."

"We *are* doing something romantic! I *love* fishing."

"I know you're not a fisherman, Al, so why
did you bring me out with you today?"

Knightcrawler

"He's a politician's assistant. He has exceptional skill handling large mouths."

"Can't we have turkey like everyone else?"

"What are you doing playing the piano? You should be outside practicing your fly-casting."

When street construction workers go ice fishing

"It's been a great day – I've caught tons of fish and it's just beautiful out here. Oh yeah, and the captain fell overboard three hours ago."

"It was a great catch. I patched it and ran it on the family sedan for 68,000 miles."

"That wasn't leftover Chinese food, and those *certainly* weren't noodles!"

"Take me to your leader."

"As a general rule, I wouldn't recommend that plug."

"Yeah, I popped the hatch so you could oil my fishing reels, too."

There it was—a majestic beast scaling the heights
against a roaring tide. It was a mighty fin-bearer,
flinging about its foe. It was a Goliath with gills.
Its name . . . Codzilla.

"When I agreed to get a shot in exchange for a sucker, I thought . . ."

"It's either a bait shop or your family reunion."

"I don't care if it is good luck, I'm not kissing
your leech!"

"I never knew you could breed a fishing dog."

"How 'bout I just swim alongside you?"

Daddy catches a bassoon.

"Well, at least now we've provided structure."

"They're really biting today."

"That's a wall eye."

**Becky Landstrum's patented underhand cast was
the stuff of legends.**

"Here, take these . . . I'm going back for the wife!"

Ceasefire

"Truth is he kept it alive for ten weeks and fed it steroids."

"Here's your problem . . . your outboard motor
is a tackle box."

"You caught it, you clean it!"

"I really think that once you get your first bite,
you'll really eat this up."

"He's my new fish finder."

"I should have been playing basketball instead of fishing. All day long, it was nothing but net."

"Hey, hon, I found a plentiful spot over here . . .
six keepers so far!"

Gutting a fish

"Okay, take your time, Mr. Vandevold, and when you're ready, point out to me the one that got away."

"Darndest spinner bait I've ever seen."

"He's watching his favorite fishing show: his fillets are in the microwave."

"Weren't we s'posed to unhook the boat first?"

"So, I guess we'll just come back for the boat, huh?"

"Perch."

"I'm done for the day. Catch you later."

"Goin' pike fishing, eh?"

"You shoulda been here yesterday."

"Fly your own ties?"

"Don't worry, there are plenty of other fish in the sea."

"I'm hoping to catch a school."

**Fishing buddies Claude and Roy take their new
outboard for a spin.**

**Jacob responds to his pregnant wife's midnight
cravings for pickerel and ice cream.**

"So what romantic thing do *you* see in the clouds?"

"Dang it, Alfred, will ya quit dangling yer bait in front of me so close to lunchtime? It looks like a french fry!"

Betty subdues Henry the same way she handles bass.

Wilfred tiptoed delicately about, attempting to avoid spooking the fish.

Cutthroat Trout

**Tom makes an extremely rare sighting:
the belly smackerel.**

**Ricardo's about to catch his very first
screaming wedgie.**

Glenn found a way to significantly increase the distance of his casts.

With great sensitivity, Ned attempts to de-Barb the hook.

Few things in life are as beautiful as watching a son set . . . a hook, that is.

Dazed and confused astride his dinghy, in one last desperate move, Melvin decides to shoot the rapids.

"Doggone it, Horace—didn't you see the sign?"

"Something tells me it's gonna be a good day."

"You said you needed to clean the fish, so I caught you a sponge."

When lure makers go too far

"I was destined to love fishing. My ancestors were Angler-Saxons."

"Teach another to fish and you'll
never get your rod back."

"That was an uneventful catch . . . generally, I like
a little more action."

Fly Fisherman

"I caught it off a deserted isle . . . aisle 15 in
the Fishing Pro Shop."

Fishermen's pier pressure

"Whoops, sorry about where I dropped the live bait, Grandpa!"

"But the sign said the limit was 55!"

"It's clear to me, Mr. Denney—you're a wormaholic."

"Do you want flies with that?"

"Boy, that last meal stuck to the roof of my mouth."

"I believe in global worming."

"Now what were you saying about a
great leader?"

"What's the matter? Haven't you ever seen a salmon run before?"

"The last thing I remember before my head hit the pier was the sound of fish laughing."

"I doubt that your brother even notices that we're not at his wedding."

"I caught it at the Finger Lakes."

"Now, this is quality time!"

"He said to throw anything back that wasn't up to standard."

"Wait a minute—you fried my lure!"

"She was the one that got away—but not far enough away."

"You're right, Marty—he's a keeper."

"Yeah, the first lunker is always special."

"Tag. You're it."

A fine line separates a very patient man from a complete idiot.

"That one was three feet, easy."

"It's always easy to tell which one is the best fisherman."

When God restocks rainbow trout streams

"When you said, 'Tie the knot,' I thought we were going fishing."

"This isn't what I had in mind when you said you'd take me line dancing."

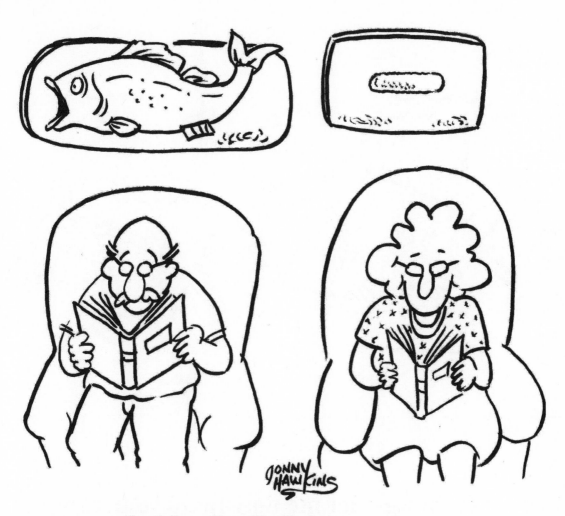

In Mrs. Paul's living room

"Hold up—let me download something
online real quick."

"I'll be your waders today."

"They're biting down at the power plant—
on glowworms."

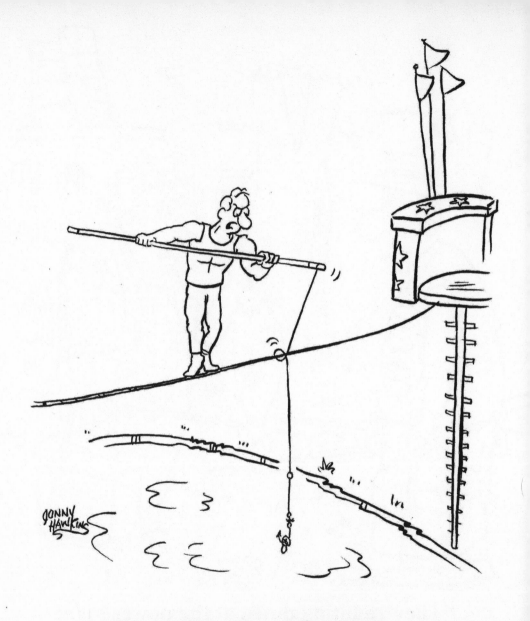

When high wire walkers fish

"They're biting on woolly boogers."

Fishing with Pinocchio

Worminator: Revenge of Nature

"Billy, just pretend it's a monster catfish under your bed."

"Are you kidding?! Cutbait?!"

"We've got to get out of here! What can
we do to make him kick the bucket!?"

"Don't be silly—you can't get salmonella from salmon!"

"Give a man a fish, you have fed him for today. Teach a man to fish and he'll be gone the whole weekend."

"Wanna fire up my hybrid motor?
It'll literally take your breath away."